HORSES FOR COURSES

HORSES FOR COURSES

A Beginner's Guide

Written by

Russell S. Stokes

Senior Jockey
Forty years' experience in the international racing industry

Edited by

Shane D. Ryan

University of New England
Armidale, New South Wales
Australia

To order additional copies of this book, contact:
Xlibris
1-800-455-039
www.Xlibris.com.au
Orders@Xlibris.com.au
768901

CONTENTS

ABOUT THE AUTHOR

THIS IS THE first book by new author Russell S. Stokes. Russell has extensive knowledge of horses; his background includes horse racing, competing as an international rider, and educating beginner horse riders. Furthermore, Russell has over four decades of experience with horses, teaching as a qualified horse riding instructor, jockey, trainer, conditioner, and horsebreaker. As an international expert, Russell's skills and knowledge have led him to travel the globe, including locations such as Japan, New Caledonia, Singapore, Malaysia, as well as many towns across Australia. He utilised these opportunities to educate others whilst expanding his own knowledge.

He began his career in the late 1960s as a stable hand in Sydney, Australia. Russell's potential was spotted early, and he quickly achieved the position of trainee jockey. In 1971, whilst based in north-west New South Wales, Russell was promoted to apprentice jockey, achieving a record of 116 wins from 776 race rides. During 1972 to January 1976, Russell was awarded the title of champion apprentice by the North North West Racing Association (NNWRA).

In three consecutive racing seasons, he was named champion apprentice at the Quirindi track, New South Wales. As a result of Russell's successful record during his time as an apprentice, Russell completed his apprenticeship in January 1976. From 1976 to 1986, Russell travelled overseas, successfully competing as a senior jockey internationally.

During this time, Russell was contracted by Mr Lucien Babin and the Jockey Club to ride in races in New Caledonia. As a professional jockey, Russell Stokes has a total record of 309 wins from 2,460 starts. Russell's passionate love of horses then drew his attention to working behind the scenes, working with horse studs throughout Australia and Japan.

Quirindi track presentation, 1973.

After nearly two decades of active competition, Russell decided that his time as a jockey had come to an end, and in 1986, he retired. Taking some time off from the horse industry, Russell worked repairing houses around his hometown. However, in January 1995, Russell moved to Gympie, Queensland, gaining employment riding track work and in barrier trials. During this time, Russell was involved in an accident in which a horse threw its rider and crashed into his horse, in the process breaking his left leg, a compound fracture.

This left Russell in a plaster cast for six months and off work for fourteen months. Upon recovering from this injury, Russell decided, 'If I am going to ride horses again. With the possibility of injury, I might as well return to racing.' In 1998, Russell returned to the track, competing as a senior jockey in the Queensland horse racing circuit. Now back in the horse industry, Russell quickly established himself as an educated veteran of the sport. As a result, Russell was again offered opportunities internationally.

In 1999, Russell worked as a horsebreaker and educator for Nakamura Chikusan P/L in Hokkaido, Japan. After his nine-month working period had ended, he returned home to Australia. However, after a short time, he again returned to Japan, this time working at the KI Farm for two six-month periods as well as one three-month period. Between the period of November 2002 and February 2003, Russell's expertise was enlisted by Komatsu Onsen Bokujo on the island of Honshu, Japan. It was here that Russell decided his riding days were over. Instead, he decided to become an educator, passing on his vast wealth of knowledge to the staff, assisting with the breaking in of young horses.

Stelus Shot, my favourite horse, at Nakamura Chikusan P/L.

Between the years of 2003 and 2013, Russell continued working in racing stables as well as teaching in horse riding schools, such as

Welcome Horse Riding Centre, The Lonely Pony Riding Centre and The McIntyre Centre. This further honed his skills as an educator, allowing him to attain more experience through teaching opportunities.

Russell completed his correspondence course with HorseRidingCoach.com in Brisbane, while in Japan, returning home he began training as a Horse riding Instructor in 2003, and completed his training in 2006. His expertise was again requested in Japan by Mr. Maekawa from Mitsubishi Thoroughbred Training Centre for short stints in 2013 and 2015. Teaching staff Breaking In skills, during the winter months. Russell continued to work in the Australian horse industry until 2016. When Russell again traveled internationally to Punggol Ranch in Singapore, Russell became a Stable manager, with over 60 horse in his care, however after 3 months of service, he decided to return home to Australia.

With over four decades of experience in the industry, Russell has acquired a broad base of theoretical knowledge as well as established a strong background in the practical understanding of horses. Furthermore, Russell is a qualified trail-riding instructor, equine deep-muscle therapist, and basic equestrian coach. Russell travelled the globe for over four decades, honing his craft; he worked in racing stables and horse riding schools. As an educator, it is Russell's ambition to teach apprentice jockeys and track riders his knowledge. Drawing on his many years of experience to help future jockeys and horse riders, this book enlists his skills as an educator to deliver an easy-to-understand beginner's horse riding book.

Russell Stokes, 1983, New Caledonia.

ACKNOWLEDGEMENTS

I WOULD LIKE to take this opportunity to thank my family. Their love and support, both financial and personal, have allowed my dreams to become reality. My late father, Russell Stokes; mother, Margaret; as well as sisters, Judi Cox and Jennifer Ryan, have all played an important role in my life. Sister Judi provided much-needed support through the hardest points of my life, and I would like to especially acknowledge her contribution to my career.

Additionally, I would like to thank my teachers Marion and Bert Hartog. Their support and encouragement in the early years of my career helped shape the experiences of my life as well as helped to develop my knowledge of horses. Their coursework and their patience and skill as teachers provided the tools necessary for a rather impatient student to learn.

A special thank you to my practical-training teachers, Linda Perkins and Ken Dagley, at Welcome Horse Riding. Without their teaching, I'd have never made it to this stage of my career. Liz Brown, manager at Welcome Horse Riding, helped develop my dressage skills, encouraged my development, as well as became a valued friend.

Julie Porter from Lonely Pony, I'd like to thank you for giving my career its beginning. Gaining employment at the Lonely Pony provided a stepping stone for my career. This position further established my teaching skills to develop further through real-life experiences. Working at Lonely Pony provided my first opportunity to teach groups of students, as previously I had only experienced one-on-one private lessons.

Also I would like to take this opportunity to thank my Japanese friends, the Nakamura family at Nakamura Chikusan P/L and KI Farm in Hokkaido, Japan, as well as all my friends at Komatsu Onsen Bokujo in Honshu, Japan. In addition, I would like to thank everyone at Mitsuishi Thoroughbred Training Centre, Hokkaido, Japan. Working overseas helped open up my skills, expand my knowledge, and assist with the further development of my teaching skills.

Special mention goes to my daughter Julieanne 'Mary' Monteith. Mary's management skills and knowledge of publishing processes were vital assets. As a result, without her assistance, this book would not have become a reality.

CHAPTER 1
BUYING YOUR FIRST HORSE

I N MY CAREER, I have learnt many valuable lessons; the following advice comes from decades of experience and can assist in choosing the correct horse for you. When looking to buy your first horse, ensure that you take someone with you that has horse knowledge. This can be anyone from a pony club instructor to a professional horse rider or anyone that can offer some form of expert advice. If you do not know anyone in the horse industry, you can ask around local pony clubs, riding schools, or stables. Members of the horse industry have valuable information and may be able to assist with finding out the horse's history. Never buy the first horse you see; instead, look around to find the best buy.

If you are a beginner rider or have only had minor riding experience, I would recommend that you enrol in a proficient riding school. The horses that you would ride at these schools would be trained, quiet, and gentle. Instructor coaches will give you all the information that you need to know in the form of a step-by-step guide to riding.

Things you need to know before buying a horse include age, size, height, and gender. You also need to know if the horse has been involved with pony clubs, equestrian work, jumping, stock work, and leisure riding or if it was a family pet. The history of the horse is very important information. Who has ridden the horse before and why? Non-horse people often think that every horse is the same; this is an incorrect assumption. Horses are very much like people. They each have their own personality. For example, they can be gentle, angry, stubborn. They have likes and dislikes similar to a human. Additionally, they may have bad habits, sicknesses, or previous injuries that may affect their suitability of being ridden. It is very important to match the rider to the horse. For example, a big person would not buy a little or skinny horse. Also, it is important to match up a rider's experience to the suitable horse. For example, you would not put a learner rider on a racehorse out of training, even if the horse was eight years old. These horses would need to be retrained by an experienced rider. I say to my students, 'You would not learn to drive a sports car or truck before first learning to drive a car.'

Oftentimes, a good horse will come up for sale because the rider has grown too big for their horse, like when children buy horses. Additionally, the previous rider may have had to leave town for work, or a child may leave for boarding school and have no use for the horse any more. A family not having the finances required to keep the horse any more, the owner giving the horse away to a good home, having no grass left in the paddock, or any other of the countless reasons that someone may choose to sell their horse—there are many causes for good horses to go up for sale. Always investigate.

When you arrange to inspect a horse, you want to witness the horse caught in the paddock, groomed, saddled up, and ridden. This will assist you, as the buyer, in observing the horse's nature and suitability. If suitable, ask for a one-month trial in the form of a written document, and pay a small deposit. Oftentimes, if the owners get the horse ready prior to the buyer's arrival, it is due to the horse having bad habits, such as jumping around and generally being naughty. The horse may have many issues that you may not see upon first inspection. For example, the horse may be hard to ride or may be difficult to control for the first few minutes of the ride.

Ask as many questions as possible about the history of the horse, including how long they have had the horse, who owned it before them, if more than one person has ridden it, the type of riding the owner has performed with the horse, when it was last wormed out, if it has ever been sick, if it has had bad injuries, and if it has been inoculated for tetanus, strangles, and so on. As an example, I heard a story once of people who had bought a horse based solely on its photo in a magazine. The horse was then sent to them. However, when the horse arrived, it had only one eye. The new owners then called the previous owner and said, 'You did not tell me that the horse had only one eye!' And the previous owner replied, 'You did not ask.' In my experience, 'Buyer beware' is a valuable quote.

As an inexperienced rider, you will see people riding a horse and oftentimes will assume that the horse is easily ridden. However, an experienced rider will make it look that way. Years of riding different horses will give you that skill. It is not acquired within the first six lessons. For example, during a teaching session in Singapore, I had been teaching two adults to ride very quiet horses. They were lazy, bombproof horses; however, the riders could not keep the horses walking, or they would stop when the riders would turn, frustrating them. At the end of the lesson, I said to the two riders, 'I will ride them one at a time and show you that they are easy to ride.' I then rode each horse around the arena whilst steering the horses in and out of the cone indicators, stopping, and walking off again. The two riders could not believe how easy it looked to them, to which I replied, 'The horses know that I know what I am doing.' When you have ridden thousands of different horses in different parts of the world at the highest level of competition, you gain many different skills. This experience gives you the ability to feel the horse's movement, through your body and through the reins, before it stops.

When you begin riding, make sure you have a safe yard in which to practise your steering as well as your stop-and-go techniques. Perform these at a walking pace to begin with. This will allow you to get the skill correctly first. This way, your control and balance will develop without serious accidents. All riders fall off at some point. It will happen, and usually with beginner riders, it's a balance issue. However, do not give up; balance comes with time and practice. Throughout my career, I have had many falls. It was never my idea. But it comes with the job. As a horse person, you will fall. The number 1 rule is, always wear a riding helmet!

Have fun, and learn as I have learnt. I often say to young riders, 'If you learn your craft well, you will be able to get work anywhere in the world.' The work will come as you learn. For example, a student of mine volunteered at a local riding school at the age of fourteen. As a result, at the age of seventeen, she gained employment at racing stables, riding racehorses.

My First Horse

Russell Stokes, pony Gypsy, and sister Jennifer, 1967.

Russell bought his first horse from his auntie Carol. Carol then gave Russell a three-minute riding lesson, and then he was on his own. From there, Russell taught himself to ride. Back then, there were no riding instructors, so Russell's only option was to practise. From the age of twelve, Russell knew he wanted to be a jockey. He describes himself as a real horse lover.

Russell Stokes on Highland Sun after winning his first barrier trial at age fifteen, 1969, Rosehill, Sydney.

CHAPTER 2

HELPFUL HINTS

Horses Pulling Back

I F A HORSE is pulling back whilst you are leading it, do not pull against it. Instead, in a calming voice, talk to the horse whilst letting your lead rope loose. Then slowly walk up to the horse's shoulder; speak softly to the horse, as this will calm it down. Furthermore, give the horse a rub or pat on its shoulder or neck as it stands. Also, rub the soft part of its nose to reassure the horse that it is okay. Often the wind will stir the horse up, or it may be another horse running around the paddock. Many things can spook a horse.

Natural Aids

Aids refer to the natural point of contact between the rider and the horse, for example, legs, seat, hands, as well as voice commands. *Voice commands* refer to the verbal commands of the rider to the horse, such as 'Whoa!' 'Steady!' 'Pick up!' or 'Stop!'

Artificial Aids

If a horse is lazy or stubborn, whips or spurs are used to encourage working at the required rate. For example, these artificial aids are used in paces as well as transitions from walk to trot to canter, if required.

Poisoning: Lantana Plant

Upon suspicion that your horse may have consumed a toxic plant, you must first inspect the horse's gum colour. Upon inspection, a horse suffering the effects of poisoning will have gums of a blotchy colour, with various spotty shades of pink and red. Furthermore, the horse's body language will often show signs of an issue with the horse's health. To medicate this issue, give the horse an injection of approximately twenty millilitres of vitamin C. Repeat if required. This will counteract the toxins of the plant. Then allow the horse to rest and give it plenty of water and hay. After two days, the horse should have no remaining symptoms. Furthermore, you can utilise paraffin oil and bran mash to flush the toxins through the system quicker to further relieve the problem. If problems persist, contact your local veterinary clinic.

CHAPTER 3
BASIC POINTS OF A HORSE

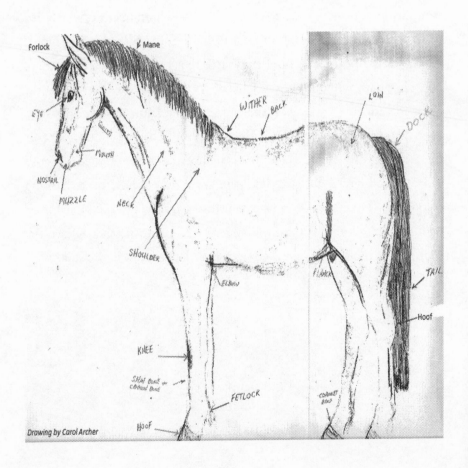

Drawing by Carol Archer

CHAPTER 4
MARKINGS ON YOUR HORSE: KNOWING THE GENDER

O
FTEN, THE TERMS used by experienced riders can become confusing to a beginner rider. The following are the terms used within the horse industry as well as the names given to horses with specific observable characteristics (for example, a horse's age and gender can affect the correct terminology for that horse):

- colt: young male horse up to the age of three years old, unmarked and not gelded
- stallion: male, four years old or older, unmarked and not gelded
- rig: male, with only one testicle down, can be any age
- gelding: male, marked, castrated, can be any age
- filly: female, up to three years old
- mare: female, over four years old.

The following terms are used to identify specific characteristics of a horse based on the location of the marks as well as the style of the marks on the horse. Often utilised by people within the horse industry to describe a horse, these terms are invaluable and must be learnt by any beginner rider.

The following are terms related to markings on the horse's legs:

- sox: white hair that goes to just past the fetlock area
- stockings: white hair that goes up to and beyond the knees and hock area
- ermine marks: black or chestnut hair inside the white mark on the legs.

The following are terms related to markings on the horse's face:

- star: a white mark on the forehead, from small to large circular shapes of hair, between the eyes and above; some can even look similar to a diamond shape
- stripe: a thin white mark down the face that goes to the nostril, which can have a 'star' joining it between the eyes (star and stripe)
- blaze: a wider white mark that stays between the eyes and nostrils in width; it can go down to the top lip
- white/baldy face: white mark that covers most of the face; the shapes of these marks can vary in design
- snip: a white mark around the nostril area
- NB: markings of a star, broken strip, and snip, which are not joined.

The following are general terms related to the horse's base coat:

- Black and brown: These colours are two tones, as the genes which decide a horse's coat were too closely aligned. This is the same for horses with a bay-and-brown base coat.
- Bay: The colour can be different shades of bay, from light bay (tan) to a deep bay red in colour. There are black points or a black mane and tail with white markings at times.
- Chestnut: This is a tone of red to deep red, bronze, copper, and even yellow. Chestnut horses can also have chestnut manes and tails as well as yellow and blonde manes and tails. They can also have white markings on their coat.
- Grey: Grey horses can be born with a different-coloured coats: chestnut, brown, black, or bay. As they mature, a more prominent grey coat comes through. They can be a mixture of colours. Grey horses will often have a grey mother (dam) or father (sire).
- Steel grey: Blue and grey hair will go completely grey as the horse matures.

The above photo is an example of a chestnut filly by Forty-Niner, one of my breakers, at Nakumura Chikusan P/L, Japan.

CHAPTER 5
YOUR HORSE'S HEALTH AND CARE

THIS CHAPTER INCLUDES valuable information regarding horse health and horse care. The information included within this chapter is gathered from decades of experience and could be the difference between a healthy horse and an unhealthy horse. For example, the following are observable signs of a healthy horse and an unhealthy horse:

Healthy Horse

- ❖ The horse has a bright and shiny coat; coat length depends on the season and breed of the horse.
- ❖ The eyes are bright and clear.
- ❖ The horse's manure should break up on contact with the ground.
- ❖ Urine colour should be clear; it should not be thick and syrupy.
- ❖ The horse has good appetite.
- ❖ Gum colour should be a salmon-pink colour.
- ❖ There's no heat in the legs or feet.
- ❖ Body condition looks full and healthy but not overweight.

❖ Heartbeat has a clear and constant beat, thirty to forty-five beats per minute at rest.

❖ The horse is alert and willing to work.

❖ The horses is gently swishing its tail around whilst at rest.

❖ The horse runs in the paddock and is being social with other horses.

❖ Standing head to tail, the horses rustle flies away from their fellow horses. I often refer to this as the horse's version of the old adage, 'You scratch my back, and I will scratch yours'. Furthermore, horses love contact with other horses, not unlike humans. However, horses also love to have fun on their own at times or with their social group and sometimes with humans. They will do things that allow them to relax and unwind.

❖ The horse rolls for fun, shaking the dirt or grass off.

❖ The horse lies in the sun (sunbaking).

❖ The horse sleeps standing, bottom lip drooping.

❖ The horse stands in the sun or shade, resting a hind leg.

❖ The horse scratches its back or rear on a fence or tree.

❖ While standing in the water, the horses splashes itself or other horses.

❖ The horse rolls in the mud. Horses often do this as when the mud dries, it acts as a type of natural blanket, keeping them warm at night.

❖ The horse gets physical with other horses, kicking each other. This may look violent, but they are often just having fun.

Unhealthy Horse

❖ The horse has a dull coat.

❖ The horse has sad or weeping eyes.

❖ The coat has skin complaints—for example, Queensland itch, rain scalds, and so on.

❖ The horse is in poor condition: hips or ribs protruding, overly skinny.

❖ There is ear discharge or possible ear infection or mites in the ear.

❖ The nose has a thick discharge.

❖ The horse is rubbing the dock of the tail—possible worm problem or itch problem.

❖ The horse is lethargic, with little to no energy.

❖ The mane and tail have been rubbed out—possible itch.

❖ The horse is overweight, which can cause laminitis (found in the feet)

❖ There are signs of pain, agitation, or aggression.

❖ There are injuries, wounds, or infections.

❖ The horse has abdominal pain—possible colic.

❖ The horse has diarrhoea (caused by bacteria), heavy worm infestations, or stress.

❖ The horse is off its feed, not eating.

Note: Stress can be a major contributing factor to the health of a horse. The causes of stress can be as simple as the horse working too hard, too quick. For example, the horse may bolt with their rider before they have the fitness to do so, which would overstress the heart.

CHAPTER 6

GROOMING GEAR

To PROPERLY CARE for your horse, you will need to ensure that you maintain your horse's hygiene. To achieve this, you will require the appropriate grooming kit to ensure that your horse remains healthy and happy. The following are the equipment one would expect to find in a horse's full grooming kit:

❖ dandy brush
❖ curry comb
❖ body brush
❖ two sponges
❖ towel
❖ scraper
❖ mane comb
❖ hoof pick
❖ disinfectant
❖ shampoo and conditioner
❖ plastic bucket
❖ wisp
❖ rubber bands
❖ scissors

- ❖ bot knife
- ❖ Vaseline
- ❖ baby oil
- ❖ oil pot or tar pot
- ❖ hoof brush
- ❖ lambswool gloves.

Pictured above is a basic grooming kit.

Dandy brush. This brush has very stiff bristles that are fairly long. This brush is mostly used to brush manes and tails out.

Curry comb or hand mitten. This is used to clean mud or dry dirt out of a horse's coat. The brush also removes old hair; horses often enjoy this experience as it gently massages the body. Do not brush over bony areas. Furthermore, to prevent dirt and hair from clogging up the comb, ensure that you regularly tap it against a solid surface to clean.

Body brush. This is a very soft brush and is also used for brushing dirt out of the horse's coat. When using this brush, ensure that you have a damp sponge or towel nearby. Then every couple of brush strokes, wipe the dirty brush over the sponge or towel. This will remove the dirt and clean the brush. Furthermore, when brushing, flick your wrist to the left in each stroke. This will assist in removing the old hair and dirt out of the coat more effectively. Additionally, establish a routine of long firm strokes as this is the most effective method.

Two sponges. One is used to clean the horse's bottom and dock of the tail. The second sponge is used to shampoo the body, legs, and head. Additionally, you can choose just to sponge-wash your horse after a workout.

Towel. This is used to dry your horse after washing and can also be used to gloss their coat up after a body brush.

Scraper. This can be plastic or hoop iron. This is used to remove water after being washed. It can also be used to remove sweat from the horse's coat. However, this tool is only suitable for the muscly areas of the horse's body.

Mane comb. This tool is used to pull the mane and to get knots out of the mane. This tool is much larger than a regular comb.

Hoof pick. This is used to clean out dirt, manure, and mud from the bottom of the horse's feet.

Disinfectant. This is used for eliminating germs and bacteria from a horse's coat, mane, and tail. It is also used to clean brushes after use.

Shampoo and conditioner. This is used to clean the horse's coat, mane, and tail and to clean equipment prior to disinfecting.

Water. This is used for washing, cleaning, and diluting disinfectants.

Small plastic bucket or wisp bucket. This is used for cleaning the horse as well as cleaning equipment.

Wisp towel. This is used for cleaning the horse's body, legs, and face. Dampen prior to use.

Rubber band. This is used to tie the plaits in the horse's mane.

Scissors. This is used for trimming the mane, bridle area, and winter hair.

Bot knife. This is used for cleaning off botfly eggs.

Vaseline. This is used to grease a stallion's testicles and is used for racehorses to highligh the horse's eyes and its muzzle area.

Baby Oil. This is wiped over the eyes and muzzle area to highlight the face. Place a few drops in clean water, with the wisp in the water. Then wring your wisp towel out well and wipe your clean brush with the towel. This will gloss your horse's coat up.

Oil pot or tar pot. This is used to prevent cracked or brittle feet. This is achieved by painting the mixture on the sole, frog area, and top of the hoof. Modern-day methods for achieving this involve medicated hoof oil, tar, or cooking oil. Past techniques involved sump oil or a mix of melted-down mutton fat and tar.

Hoof brush. This is used for washing the dirt and mud from under and around the sole area of the hoof. Hoof brushes are also used for scrubbing mud off the horse and cleaning track gear, girths, surcingles, and so on.

Lambswool gloves. This is used to polish off a horse's coat.

Note: If a horse has a skin problem, such as an itch, the issue can be transferred via a contaminated brush or other forms of grooming equipment that comes in contact with a horse's skin. Furthermore, if the horse is not healthy, its appearance will not improve. An unhealthy horse will always look unhealthy. A former boss of mine, Arthur Gore, often used to say, 'Son, if they're healthy on the outside, then they are healthy on the inside.' The moral of this story is that if a horse appears health, then it usually is. The opposite is also true.

CHAPTER 7
GROOMING LESSON

Natural spring spa at Komatsu Onsen Farm, Japan.

THE FOLLOWING IS a step-by-step guide to the process of grooming your horse. These techniques are innovated from over four decades of experience and have been thoroughly tested and found to be the most effective method when grooming your horse. Follow this step-by-step guide to ensure appropriate and effective care as well as to maintain your horse's hygiene.

It is important that the horse is safely secured at all times during the grooming process. Ensure that you have the appropriate grooming kit available. Revisit Chapter 6 for appropriate grooming kit equipment.

During the winter or colder months, it is only appropriate to wash the horses in the middle of the day as this is often the warmest time. Also, it is vital to note that it is never appropriate to wash a horse that is sick or unwell. This is due to their immune system already being weakened, thus increasing their risk of contracting a virus, flu, or other illness.

Furthermore, if a horse is unrugged, never wash them. The reason for is this: a rugged horse will regain their body heat after getting washed; however, an unrugged horse is unable to achieve this due to the process of washing their coat, which removes the natural oils that protect them from the elements. For example, the natural oils on an unrugged horse assist in keeping the horse warm in cold rainy weather by repelling water. The coat is water-resistant due to the natural oils produced.

Once the horse is secured and you have gathered your grooming kit, you may begin to groom your horse. If the horse is dirty or has dried mud clumps on its legs, take one sponge and wash its legs down, breaking the lumps of mud up. Then when that is finished, you can clean out your horse's feet whilst their legs are drying.

To safely perform this task, stand at the left-hand side of the horse near the side shoulder, run your left hand down the leg, place your hand around the fetlock, put pressure with your elbow on the back of the knee, and say, 'Pick up.' Then with your right hand, clean out the hoof with the hoof picker. After you have cleaned the hoof to a satisfactory standard, tap the shoe with the picker. This will remove the dust out of the shoe area.

It is important that you do not touch the frog and always clean the dirt out from the back of the shoe, ensuring that when using the picking tool, you are always working away from yourself to prevent injury. Furthermore, it is vital that you are always working towards the toe of the shoe. Upon completion, gently let the foot down, ensuring that your own feet are away from that area.

After cleaning the hooves, with the curry comb in hand, start at the horse's neck area. Ensure that you work your curry comb in a circular motion, using the comb only on the muscly areas and avoiding the bony areas. Work towards the back of the horse. As you need to clean your comb, hit it on the stable wall to free the dirt and mud from the comb. Then dip the comb in the water bucket to clean it. The rubber will grip the loose hair out as you work the circular motion.

Keep the other hand on the horse. This will allow you to feel if the horse goes to move or attempt to kick you as it will move quicker. To minimise this risk, talk to your horse whilst you work. Follow the same process when cleaning the opposite side of the horse. Be careful around the flank and belly area as the horse may be ticklish.

When working around the leg area of the horse, use your dampened hands, and run them down around the legs as well as towards the back of the legs. This will remove loose hairs; you can clamp your hand and give the horse a good massage. This will assist in removing the sweat and dirt build-up and at the same time relaxing the horse. Then use a damp wisp towel and start at the neck, moving your hand in a circular motion. Again, do this with one hand working and the other remaining in contact with the horse to ensure safety. Remember to constantly speak to the horse; this will calm the horse and allow it to know where you are so as to not spook the horse. As the wisp loses moisture, remember to rinse the towel out so as to keep it damp. Now it is time to move on to the legs, ensuring that you squat to work and never sit down. Then begin to work the damp towel up and down the legs, ensuring to give the heels a good clean also.

Collect the body brush and the damp towel. To clean the brush, I rub it over the damp towel. It is very important to correctly clean your brush as you will not clean a horse with a dirty brush. Start brushing from the neck area, working down the neck, the front legs, back to the withers, along the body, then under the belly, up and over the rump, then down the hind leg. Then repeat the process on the opposite side, ensuring that you always follow the flow of the coat. At the flank, you change directions a couple of times. After that, give the head a gentle brush; follow the hair lines around the ears. Upon completion, brush out the mane, tail, and forelock next with a dandy brush. Often, the tail will have matted knots in it, and you will need to use your fingers to pull out the knots. Next, get a clean dry towel and wipe over the coat. Always follow the flow of the coat. After drying the horse, check and treat any injuries, wounds, or cuts. Finally, paint oil on all four hooves to prevent cracking of the feet or a brittle foot.

Note: During wintertime, the coat is more dense and harder to keep clean. In addition, under the belly around the girth area, a build-up of sweat can give them a sore back around the saddle areas as well as under the front legs. Furthermore, dirt and sweat can also build up around the head where the bridle fits to the horse.

CHAPTER 8
CLEANING FEET OUT SAFELY

ADOPTING THE CORRECT methods for cleaning the feet of your horse will allow a rider to perform this essential task safely and efficiently. Firstly, tie the horse up in a safe location and stand at the nearside from shoulder with the hoof pick in your right hand. Then face the back of the horse and run your left hand down the back of the horse's front leg. Use your elbow to apply pressure on the back of the horse's knee; this will result in the horse lifting its front foot up. You may now begin cleaning around the shoe, ensuring to always work the pick away from your body so as to avoid injury. Then give the shoe a tap with the pick to get rid of the dust from the cleaning process. Put the foot down gently, and watch that the horse does not put its foot down on your toes.

Upon completion, move to the horse's hind leg. In theory, the process of cleaning the rear feet is rather similar. To begin, run your hand down the hind leg and say, 'Pick up.' Support the hind leg on your hand area. Once you feel ready, work the pick down and away from your body. Give the shoe a tap to loosen the dust. Then let the leg down slowly, ensuring to guide the leg away from your own feet.

To continue, move around behind the horse with your hand on the horse and talk in a calming voice to ensure the horse is aware of your location. Move to the offside shoulder and repeat the steps from the nearside, with the only change being that the pick is now in your left hand and your right hand runs down the back of the horse's leg.

Note: Sometimes when you are trying to pick the horse's feet up, they will be resting a leg. To solve this, you may need to push them up straight. This will get them standing. Always be aware that your horse is concentrating on what you are doing, and at times, they may get a little restless. Finally, it is vital that you always have good footwear on your feet when around horses.

It is recommended that you always clean out the horse's feet prior to working them. This is to prevent stones or dry mud from putting pressure on the frog or the sole of the foot. In the Australian horse industry, it is common practice to put oil under the sole of the hoof and to paint oil on top of the hoof, finishing just below the coronet line. In contrast, in Japan, it is common practice to only oil the outside (top) area. When cleaning out the hoof, ensure that you are constantly checking as to whether there are any shoe problems, for example, loose shoe, nails damaged, cracks, and/or other injury or defect.

CHAPTER 9
GEAR CHECK

ENSURING THAT YOUR gear is properly maintained and stored can be the difference between long-lasting functional equipment and poor-performing gear. Firstly, the bridle must fit the horse's head correctly, and the bit has to be the right fit for the horse. To check this, the horse must have a nice smile with the bit, not too loose or too tight. Then check the condition of the saddle, stirrup leathers, and girth to ensure that there are no stitching faults or wear.

Following this, check that the saddlecloth is fitting correctly, covering the back and withers so that there are no rubbing or pinching problems. Ensure that the saddlecloth is raised in the gullet of the saddle. Inspect the condition of all stitching. Make sure it is in good order with the leather, having no visible faults as well as ensuring that the noseband is fitted correctly and not cutting off the horse's breathing, if the bridle has one. Then check that the gear is all fitted.

Also ensure that all buckles and keepers are correctly fitted with no damage to this gear. The horse must be tied up safely at all times, with a string and a correctly fitted safety release. Furthermore, boots and bandages must be fitted correctly to suit it's worked out and safely on the correct leg, buckles to the back as well as the Velcro strap pulled to its back. The reins must have good grip, and if there are buckles, a keeper is used to stop the rings or the martingale from catching on the buckle during turns.

This would result in the reins putting pressure on the horse's mouth if the ring catches on the buckles. The rider must ensure that the stitching is of good quality, with the girth to be even on each side of the saddle flap and not pitching the horse. Finally, the rider must always wear appropriate clothing: riding boots and helmet. The rider must not be wearing any jewellery.

Note: Your gear has to be in good condition, with the leather well oiled with no rips or holes as well as elastic and in good order.

CHAPTER 10
SAFETY FACULTIES FOR PADDOCKS, FENCES, AND STABLES

Happy horses relaxing after working hours at Welcome
Horse Riding, Mount Samson, Queensland.

T O ENSURE THE safety of your horse, be aware that you must provide a safe and secure environment in which to house your horse. The following chapter gives examples of the types of enclosures available, their benefits, as well as their drawbacks.

Furthermore, this chapter will allow you the opportunity to select the appropriate enclosure for your horse from an educated position.

To begin with, make sure there is no rubbish, car wrecks, parts of old fences, or various other forms of litter in your paddock. Check for boggy ground near creeks and dams as well as rabbit holes, tree stumps, and dangerous or inadequate fencing. Then, lead your horse around the boundary of the paddock as well as where the water is located. Allow the horse sufficient daylight to get his bearings. For example, do not take your horse to the new paddock, where it could possibly injure itself, just before or during night-time.

- ❖ *Barbed wire.* This is very unsafe for horses. This is due to the fact that horses will often play over the fence. For example, the grass may be greener on the other side of the fence, or the horse may socialise with horses on the other side of the fence. However, the barbs can become the cause for major damage to the horse's rugs, mane, and tail.

- ❖ *Wooden post and pickets with plain wire.* This is far less dangerous to horses than barbed wire. However, the wire can still do damage to the horse's legs as they can get caught up in the wires. In addition, pickets can be sharp, and horses playing with other horses over the fence have been known to impale themselves on these pickets. To prevent this, always ensure that your pickets are safely capped to prevent injuries. The top wire on these fence types should be white; this is so the horses can clearly identify the boundary.

- ❖ *Post and rail.* This type of fencing is very safe for your horse. However, this type of fencing is rather expensive and requires frequent maintenance. This high maintenance is due to the horses leaning or rubbing against it as well as horses often chewing on this type of fencing. Additionally, horses chewing on this type of fencing can have an adverse effect on the horse's health. Note: Ensure that the spacing between the rails is not large enough for the horse to squeeze its head through and also that the bottom rail is more than twenty centimetres from ground level. This is to avoid injury to the horse. For example, horses can roll and get their feet caught underneath.

❖ *Electric fences.* In my experience, this is the safest and most effective method of fencing for horse enclosures. It is relatively cheap to erect once you have your initial electrical unit. The horses would soon grow accustomed to the electrical shock and will not play or lean over the fence. This will ensure that there is never much pressure on the wire. There are many different types of indicator tape available; using this on the fencing will ensure that the boundary is clearly visible for the horses, and it is also quiet neat. Furthermore, electric fences can be relocated easily, when necessary. Additionally, these types of fencing are relatively low-maintenance, with the only maintenance being controlling the grass and weeds underneath the fencing, therefore preventing the leak of electricity and making the fencing less effective. A cheap way of utilising existing fencing which is not quite adequate is by using outriggers and running one strand of electrified wire along the fence line. This is to ensure that the horses keep their distance from the outriggers, away from the fence.

Horses need good pasture and water supply as well as shady trees for protection.

After choosing the appropriate fencing for your paddock, another important process involves the building of a stable. A stable is an important structure for your property and is vital to the health of your horse. The following is an appropriate guide for the building of a stable:

❖ *Size of the stable.* The size of your stable should be a minimum three by three metre area for an average-sized horse to turn around and to lie down. In addition, the stable must be tall enough so that the hot air will settle above the height of the horse. It must also be well-ventilated.

❖ *Materials.* These must be fire-retardant, with smooth finishes and no protrusions.

❖ *Walls.* The walls of a stable must go all the way to the ground. This is to prevent the horse from getting its legs stuck when it lies down. There should be nothing protruding and no sharp edges.

❖ *Floors.* Floors must be slightly sloping to allow for the drainage of water. The surface can be hard or soft, but I would advise a surface that is easy to clean.

❖ *Doors.* Doors must be wide enough for the horse to easily walk through. They must be lockable, preferably allowing the horse to see through but not allowing the horses to touch each other.

❖ *Feed bins.* They must have no sharp edges, no rust, must not be able to be tipped over, and must be made of materials that are safe for horses should the horse knock it. When selecting your feed bin, you must ensure that it is large enough to hold the required horse feed. Furthermore, in my opinion, rubber bins are best suited for this job. A car tyre turned inside out on a solid base is a great homemade solution. Steel bins are strong but tend to rust, and horses can knock the steel or cut themselves on steel much easier.

❖ *Water troughs.* There should be no sharp edges and no rust. It must be solidly mounted, easy to clean, and large enough to provide a constant supply of water to your horse.

Komatsu Onsen Farm, Japan.

CHAPTER 11
BEDDING

ORRECT BEDDING IS an important factor to consider when housing your horse. The correct bedding choice can result in a well-rested and healthy horse. However, an incorrect choice can result in unrested and often very ill horses.

Type of Bedding	Positives	Negatives
Straw	Clean Easily recyclable	Need plenty of straw each day to fill boxes and can become expensive
Sand	Can be washed Easily recyclable	Often consumed by horses, causing colic
Sawdust	Easy to obtain Can be a cheap (in some areas) alternative	Dusty at times, causing coughing
Paper (shredded)	Clean	Often consumed by horses
Wood chips	Often very expensive	Often consumed by horses, causing colic
Shavings	Easy to obtain Cheap	Can be dusty, resulting in coughing
Dry grass	Cheap Clean Easy to obtain in season	Consumed by horses and can become a problem when mixed with manure

CHAPTER 12

SAFETY AROUND HORSES

T HIS CHAPTER AIMS to demonstrate the things not to do around horses, explaining common mistakes that beginner riders often make as well as giving the correct methods used to achieve your objective safely.

Things *Not* to Do Around Horses: Safety Tips

❖ Tying a horse too low to the ground. The horse will often get their legs over the ropes, thus getting their legs trapped. Always ensure that you tie your horse up between eye and nose height.

❖ Do not tie a horse up too long or too short. The recommended length is between fifty to sixty centimetres or two feet or twenty-four inches.

❖ When working on a horse's legs and when grooming or cleaning the feet out, never sit down or kneel. Rather, squat or bend whilst working on your horse.

❖ Never wear thongs, sandals, or other forms of unsuitable footwear when around horses. Always wear appropriate footwear, with riding boots or work boots being the most suitable.

❖ Never walk up from behind a horse and touch it. Instead, talk to the horse on your approach, walking up to its shoulder before making contact with the horse, ensuring that the horse is aware of your presence and will not be startled. Always let the horse know where you are. Talk to the horse. Make it aware of where you are standing. Ensure that you speak in a calm tone of voice.

❖ When picking up a horse's foot, ensure that you take extra care not to drop them down on your own toes.

❖ Never kneel in front of a horse whilst painting oil on its hooves. Kneeling often gets you a knee in the head or gets you jumped on by the horse. Avoid this at all times.

❖ Never make sudden movements around the horse as this may startle or spook the horse. Rather, move normally, ensuring that at all times the horse knows where you are. Always talk to the horse!

❖ When grooming, be aware that the horse can be ticklish around the flank area. They may react in a way that can be dangerous. To solve this, ensure you always have one hand on the horse whilst brushing or cleaning your horse's feet out. This will ensure that you will feel the horse move, giving you enough time to avoid serious injuries.

CHAPTER 13

INSTRUCTING TO SADDLE AND BRIDLE YOUR HORSE

T
HIS CHAPTER WILL act as a complete guide to the correct methods of saddling and bridling your horse as well as outline possible safety issues for beginner riders.

The following is a brief introduction to saddling your horse, with a focus on the safety of the rider. It is essential that these instructions become second nature to any rider as if the methods are incorrectly achieved, the possibility of injuries to the rider and the horse will be increased.

The first lesson that all beginner riders must learn is that you must never stand in front of the horse whilst putting a bridle on. Instead, you must stand on the nearside at the neck. Then you must adjust the bridle straps to fit the horse's head, ensuring that you tie up the horse with a weak link and not too low, taking care that you have the bridle loose enough to get it over the horse's ears. Let the bridle out first. It being too big is not a problem to get the bridle on. Adjust once it is on the horse's head, ensuring that the bridle is tight enough to prevent it from sliding around on the horse's head.

Then saddle the horse up in an enclosed area, away from other horses. This will avoid upsetting your horse or having the other horses get in your way. Ensure that you talk to your horse when you are working with them. Make sure that the girth does not pinch the horse's skin; this can be achieved by having your tack gear in good condition. Furthermore, do not squeeze between the horse and the wall to move the horse over.

As a beginner rider, it is important to follow the correct techniques. The subsequent paragraph describes the correct methods for saddling and bridling. In the beginning, when saddling, give the horse a wipe-over with a brush or towel. Give his mane and tail a brush out as well as clean its feet out. The stirrup iron should be still up from the last ride. The last thing you do is put your irons up after each ride. The reason for this is that if you do not do it this way whilst you carry the saddle to the tack room, the irons will often crash into your shin bones.

From the nearside, put your saddlecloth up the withers. The girth and surcingle are sitting on the seat of your saddle. Then lift the saddle on the horse's back and wiggle it back a little so it sits in the right place on the withers. The saddlecloth will move a little, but that is okay. After this is correctly fitted, drop the girth and surcingle down the offside. During this process, ensure that you are talking to your horse constantly to calm them. Then carefully duck under the horse's neck, and fix the girth. Untwist if required. Adjust the girth.

You may have to let it down a little to fit the horse. Then carefully duck back under the horse and pull the girth around. Pull the girth up firmly, and have the girth about one hundred millimetre from the horse's elbow. Do the strap up; tighten the girth more. Then pull it up firm. Unclip the horse, and give the horse a little lead-around to stretch their legs. Pull their front legs straight out in front of them to make sure the girth has not pinched the horse's skin. After this, lead them back, and clip them back up to where they were standing before.

This paragraph outlines the instructions required for successfully putting a bridle on your horse. To begin with, stand on the nearside of your horse, just to the left of its neck. Then whilst facing the front of the horse, adjust the bridle to be bigger than the horse's head. If it is too small, you will have trouble. Do this in a safe confined area so as to secure the horse.

With the top of the bridle in your right hand and the bit in your open left hand, place the bit up to the horse's mouth and lift the top of the bridle up over the horse's head over its closest ear. If the horse will not open its mouth, with the bit still in your left hand, put your left thumb behind its bridle tooth. It will then open its mouth. After this, place the top of the bridle over the other ear.

Pull the forelock out of the bridle, and adjust the bridle to fit this horse's head. Furthermore, there should be a crease in the horse's mouth from the bit. This cress makes the horse look like it is smiling. Then do up the throat lash, ensuring that you have a space of about four fingers between the strap and the jaw. Then place the reins over the horse's neck, and buckle them up.

CHAPTER 14

WHAT BEGINNER RIDERS NEED TO KNOW: COACHING TIPS

THIS CHAPTER IS essential reading for anyone who is interested in being involved with horses. This chapter outlines Russell Stokes's methods for coaching beginner riders. These methods have been fine-tuned by decades of experience. Topics that are covered in this chapter include coaching tips, common mistakes, mounting methods, saddling techniques, information regarding the adjusting and use of the reins, as well as balance and control skills.

The following are coaching tips that relate to the basic instruction of students in the horse industry. To begin with, explain how to approach a horse in a stable or yard. Ensure that the student is aware of the fact that they must always talk to the horse on approach, then move to his shoulder for first contact with the horse. Then teach the student how to correctly put a head collar or bridle on a horse. Couple this with teaching the student to tie a horse up in a stable wash bay or horse float, with a quick release and string as a weak link in case of a problem. In addition, demonstrate how to lead a horse on the nearside at the horse's shoulder as well as explain how to put on a rug, saddlecloth, and a saddle. Have the student lead a horse into a stable paddock; demonstrate how to turn the horse around with its head back at the gate or door before releasing. Also, educate the student on the correct mounting techniques together with techniques regarding holding the reins correctly, teaching them how to turn left and right and how to stop the horse. Then explain how to get the horse to move forward and how to sit with the ears, shoulders, hips, and heels all in a line. Finally, teach your student how to ride at a trot and a canter in rhythm with the horse, holding on to the monkey grip or saddle to get balance. There are many basic skills that students will need to learn to ride confidently; however, this can serve as a guideline for future coaches.

Mistakes commonly performed by beginner riders often involve incorrectly mounting their horse. For example, inexperienced riders often hold on to the cantle of the saddle or have their hands too far up the horse's neck or too far apart. All these things will make the saddle slip around the horse's belly when trying to mount up. Furthermore, if you cannot mount the horse by yourself, get someone to hold on to the horse, and use mounting step to assist you in gaining more height to mount the horse safely.

As an instructor or coach, ensure that you have control of the horse when mounting. Do not let go of the reins when mounting. Also ensure that when horses are lined up, keep them apart one and a half lengths to avoid being kicked. The instructor should line all riders on the centre line, facing the same direction one-half lengths apart. One at a time, the coach holds each horse whilst the rider mounts up.

On command after all the horses have been mounted, keep your distance walk into the arena, single file, mounting out in the open without a fence, with riders lining up behind each other. Staff members will help each other whilst keeping that safe distance of one and a half length. After all the horses are mounted, on command, the lead horse moves off. Beginner riders may require support from the instructor when mounting horses.

Note: All mounting and dismounting are done on the nearside (left side) only!

The following is an example of the correct dismounting technique. Hold on to both reins firmly in the left hand, even if your whip is in your left hand. It is not advisable to allow beginner riders to carry a whip until they gain enough experience to deal with the extra factor in dismounting. Take both feet out of the irons, and slide your right leg over the saddle as well as the horse's rump, ensuring that you take care not to kick the horse's rump and clear the saddle when you lift and slide your right leg over. Then both legs should be together. Slide down with both feet hitting the ground at the same time, ensuring that you bend your knees on contact to absorb the impact, lessening the strain on your knees as well as helping to keep your balance.

A second dismounting example involves holding both reins firmly in the right hand. Slide your right feet out of the irons, ensuring that you support your weight on your left iron and your arms, with the right hand still holding both reins and supported on the horse's neck. Then with your right hand on the pommel of the saddle, swing your right leg over the horse's back and rump. Clear the saddle, then move the right hand to the waist of the saddle. Have both legs together before sliding your left foot out of the stirrup iron. Then slide down to the ground, bending your knees on contact to avoid the shock of hitting the ground. Always keep your balance.

The following are a few of the common mistakes involved with dismounting that I have witnessed in my career. One of these instances involves a student leaving their left foot in the iron to dismount, hitting the ground, falling backwards, and frightening the horse. This is because the rider's legs may be too short to touch the ground. As a result, the horse takes off with a scream or just the sudden movement of the fall, causing the student to get dragged along for the ride as the foot is still stuck in the iron.

Another example of an incorrect dismount involves a student lifting their right leg over the front of the saddle and jumping off, letting go of the reins in the process. As a result, the horse gets spooked due to the sudden movement as well as the rider not lifting their leg high enough to clear the saddle or touching the horse's rump. This can be very dangerous, as a spooked horse is an unpredictable and, therefore, dangerous horse. Never put a beginner rider on flighty horses.

Educating beginner riders in the correct methods of saddling their horse can be a difficult task. This chapter shows the ways I have found most effective when instructing students. The student is shown where to stand, at the nearside shoulder area.

To adjust the girth safely, tighten the girth while facing the horse's body. Then you should have enough room to get your open hand between the horse's body and girth, ensuring that the girth strap is not twisted and the girth strap is in, with approximately four fingers' space back from the horse's elbow. Then give the horse a little walk to stretch its legs after the girth is tight so the girth will not pinch it.

Never kneel down or sit to reach under the horse's belly to get a hold of the girth strap. Some students have the girth too loose, and when they put their foot in the stirrup, the saddle may slip around. Or when girthing up, they pinch the horse's skin with the buckle they are tightening, or the horse moves and puts its hoof on the student's foot. Each rider waits for their turn in line, spaced out for their girth check from the coach.

To adjust the stirrup to your length, whilst standing on the nearside of the horse, pull the stirrup iron to the end of the leather strap as far as it will go. Then pull the end of the leather so that the bucket on the strap is about one hundred millimetres from the saddle.

Following this, put your left hand around the stitching where the buckle is located. Ensure that your thumb is held up to support the buckle firmly, and with your right hand, pull the strap straight. Then as your left hand and your thumb push away from you, let the pin slide out of the hole.

Note: They can be very stiff at times. Ensure that you are talking to the horse consistently during this process. This is so the horse knows where you are at all times. Furthermore, walk around the horse. Put your left hand on the horse's back as you walk around behind it. Let your hand stay on the horse as you guide it across the horse's rump, along its ribs, and back to the other side of the horse. Ensure that you perform no fast movements during this process. Finally, to put the buckle back to the saddle, tightly pull on the bottom strap. This will cause the buckle to slide up.

The following will educate you on the appropriate methods of measuring your stirrup leather for your own height. Firstly, start out on the nearside of the horse, facing the saddle. Follow these steps: hold the stirrup iron and strap straight out from the saddle, put the iron under your arm to touch your body, and close your fist. Then place your arm on top of the leather strap, with your knuckles touching the buckle; adjust the leather strap to this length. Do the same on the other side. It does not matter which arm you use to adjust the strap.

At all times during this process, ensure that you are talking to the horse and that you have a hand on its body so that the horse knows where you are. Common mistakes that students make involve having their hand too far away from the buckle to adjust the holes or often trying to lift the strap up and out of the hole whilst the strap is loose.

Although thought to be a seemingly simple task, it is important for beginner riders to know the correct method for safely mounting a horse. Firstly, stand at the horse's shoulder on the nearside. The left hand holds the reins, one rein over the other, resting just forward off the saddle. Ensure that the right rein is shorter than the left. This is to stop the horse from nipping at you and also to prevent the horse from spinning around as you are attempting to mount up.

Following this, place your right hand over the seat of the saddle. You should now be facing the back of the horse. Then put your left foot in the stirrup before swinging over the saddle. Often this action will require substantial momentum. To achieve the required momentum, you may have to spring off your lead foot.

Note: Counting to three is a good method for timing your movement. For example, use the first and second count to prepare yourself, and on the third count, lift yourself up and over the saddle, twisting your body to face the front of the horse. As you get up, move your right hand on to your reins. Do not flop in the saddle. Instead, sit up straight, put your right foot in the stirrup iron, look ahead, and await instructions from your coach.

Most beginner riders have difficulties with the reins on their horse. For example, a common issue involves the rider's hands slipping or when turning and not shortening up the reins again. The best way to resolve this is for the instructor to measure up the reins to the correct length for the rider and tie a knot in the reins. Correcting this issue allows the beginner rider to concentrate on learning the basics, such as bouncing to the trot, keeping their balance, and steering the horse.

In a safe yard or on a lunge lead, the rider can hold the reins with one hand, with a knot in the reins, without the stress of dropping one rein. They may also hold the saddle for balance and practise rising to a trot. Furthermore, the reins are to be held on the first knuckle in a closed fist. The ring finger has first contact to the reins. Tuck the little finger underneath the reins as it is not strong enough to hold any pressure.

The reins should come out between the thumb and the index finger; however, this may not be possible with a knot in the reins. If this is the case, the rider may be asked to keep their hand flat for now. Ensure that the rider is told not to use the reins to balance themselves as this will cause undue pressure on the horse's mouth and may cause the horse to become confused as to what the rider wants.

The beginner rider must invest the appropriate time and effort into learning the processes of horse riding. For example, a learner rider must learn the fundamentals of turning the horse, keeping their hands even down the horse's neck, and moving each rein off the horse's neck to turn left or right whilst keeping the horse moving. Also, turning your wrist down on your right hand with the reins firmly in hand is enough pressure to turn a good school horse right. The same process works for the left hand.

Note: A horse will always follow its nose. Furthermore, when riding a horse, give the horse rein. Do not choke the horse with too much pressure, as this may confuse the horse, and it will stop as well as most likely throw its head around. Never attempt to fight against the horse in these situations; instead give them a little slack then gather them up slowly.

A common mistake that beginner riders often make when learning to turn their horse is that they drop either one or both of the reins when turning. To address this issue, explain that the rider must keep their hands level and have the bit up in the horse's mouth at all times during this process. Riders often overcorrect when turning, causing them to turn the horse's neck without turning the horse. Explain to the student, 'To turn right, just move the right hand off the horse's neck and gently squeeze with your right heel, ensuring that you keep a tight grip on the reins.'

Other issues can arise from the rider, letting the horse slow down or stop whilst turning. To solve this issue, give the horse a gentle squeeze with your heel on whatever side you are on. Riders must learn to flow with the horse. Further issues can arise from beginner riders trying to steer the horse using the same methods they would use riding a motorbike; however, reins are not stiff and require different techniques. In these cases, it is important to explain to the rider that it is rather easy once they adopt the correct methods for using reins.

To appropriately educate the student, place a set of reins in their hand, with no horse attached. Then with an instructor at the opposite end of the reins, apply pressure to the reins to give the rider a better idea of the appropriate weight to place on the reins and also practise stopping methods as well as getting the student to reverse the roll back. This is a safe and effective method of educating beginner riders and can be performed as many times as necessary to practise methods of stopping and turning.

Another common issue relates to a rider's body tension, slouching in the saddle. To resolve this issue, place the rider in front of a large mirror and show them how to sit tall and proud; this is the correct method. Some riders lean forward, and their feet sit back too far as they are trying to balance. Again, put the rider in front of a large mirror and explain what they are doing incorrectly. This method works for many of the common posture mistakes of beginner riders.

As a final example, there are also riders sitting lopsided in the saddle. Again utilise the mirror reflective technique. Then the instructor will stand behind them and explain where to sit as well as how to sit straight. For example, with the lower legs too far forward and with no pressure on the stirrups, a rider will lose their balance rising to the trot and will flop back into the saddle, often slipping out of their stirrups.

Methods to resolve this issue involve checking the stirrup leather lengths as they may be too long for the rider. Kick your feet out of the stirrups, and measure the stirrup length to the rider's ankle bone. The bottom of the stirrup iron should be level with the ankle bone. This is the correct method.

CHAPTER 15

BEGINNER RIDING INSTRUCTIONS: COACHING FOR PARENTS

THESE LESSONS NEED to be performed in a safe yard with a safe horse. The following is an example of a beginner's guide to riding horses. This basic starter's lesson will work on introducing the beginner rider to the world of horse riding. To begin with, hold one rein in each hand with the rein coming from the horse's mouth. The rein should be placed between your little finger and your thumb, coming out of the top of your hand. This should look like a fist when you look down at your hands. The reins need to be in a straight line without putting pressure on the horse's mouth. Then if you put a little pressure on both of the reins, the horse will back up, if at a standstill.

If, however, this is not your desired movement, just put your hand forward with a slight loop in the reins. If after a few seconds, the horse does not respond, just wiggle your feet in the stirrup iron for a few seconds. As a result, the horse will step forward; the rider should then ease back on both reins together then rest the hands forward on the horse's mane. The horse should stand still now. Keep your feet still. Often beginner riders get nervous whilst sitting on the horse and instinctively wiggle their feet. Many do not consciously do this, but it can cause the horse to become confused, so be aware of this.

Remember, your goal from the first few lessons is to gain the ability to sit in the correct riding position—small steps until you are ready. If you are a parent giving your child an early lesson, have a lead rope on the head collar under the bridle. Many people can ride, with various levels of ability. However, the ability to teach others to ride is a different experience entirely.

For example, many riders perform the basic riding tasks instinctively, rarely thinking about a step-by-step process but rather going into a type of autopilot mode. However, when instructing your child, you must give clear-to-the-point instructions. Tell them only what they need to know. Do not overload them with too much detail; keep it simple and direct.

When you get your parents to adjust your stirrup iron, starting off on the nearside of the horse, lift your leg up so you will not pinch the inside of your leg when they pull the stirrup strap out and down to adjust the holes to your length. Then when the stirrup is adjusted and you hang your leg down, the bottom of the iron should be level with the inside of your ankle bone.

If the child is having issues with their balance, put the stirrup up about two more holes, and this will allow them to have a greater bend in their knees. When your feet are in the stirrups, the stirrups are to be on the ball of your feet, with your toes pointing in an upwards direction. Furthermore, your heels must be pointing down with your toes pointing straight ahead, not outwards like duck's feet.

Upon completion, you should be sitting in the middle of the saddle, looking straight over the horse's head, between its ears. This is the basic horse riding position.

The following is a mix of dressage and a pleasure riding position. Sitting up straight and tall, there should be a straight line in front of you. Keep your hands down on the horse's neck, unless you are turning or stopping. Your parents can line up the points for you. These hints will give you a little polish when you ride. Then with your parents standing to the side of the horse, holding the lead rope, you may ride safely; this also allows the child's riding confidence to grow through practice rather than theory.

Furthermore, whilst the horse is at a standstill, you can explain the methods used to get the horse to stop. You do not want them to practise independently until this lesson is learnt. Once you are confident that the child is ready, you can begin the lesson.

To begin, lean back slightly with your shoulder. Pull back on the reins, ensuring that you apply pressure equally to both reins. Then once the horse stops, both hands go back on to the top of the horse's neck, with no pressure on the reins. Ensure that the chid fully understands this process prior to moving to the next lesson.

The next lesson involves teaching the child to turn the horse. The lesson begins with the parent standing at the horse's left shoulder, with their left hand holding on to the side of the head collar and their right hand over the top of the child's left hand to give them an idea of the amount of pressure to apply to the reins. Then as you grip and turn the horse's head to the left, the horse will also turn its body; horses always follow their nose. Often children do not grip as they pull on the reins, and the reins slide through their fingers. This results in one rein being longer than the other.

Teaching using the methods outlined will reduce this risk as the parent is helping to turn the horse's head and then putting the child's hand back to the position it is supposed to be in, back in front of the saddle and down on the horse's neck. Repeat the exact same thing on the other side of the horse, with the only exception being that you use the opposite hands. Repeat this lesson as many times as is required for the child to understand, ensuring to talk them through the process at every lesson.

The next lesson will demonstrate how to walk forward a couple of steps and then come to a complete stop. The lesson begins with the parent holding their child's foot in the stirrup, explaining the process of wiggling the stirrup to move the horse. The parent should then wiggle the child's foot to give them an idea of the required pressure needed to get the horse to move. The horse should walk off then stop.

Note: I do not use the word *kick* with children as they often interoperate this as like kicking a soccer ball; then they kick too hard and scare the horse. Also, the horses used for these types of lessons should be reliable, calm, and bombproof.

Upon successful completion of the previous lessons, your child is ready to walk a little forward, ensuring the parent is closely by its side. Keeping a safe distance so that the horse does not walk over you, walk backwards and keep an eye on the rider. When you feel the child is ready, tell the child to wiggle both feet at the same time. Then once the horse walks off, tell the child to keep their feet still.

In this lesson, you are looking at your safety, that of the child, and that of the horse. It is recommended that the parent has the lead rope in one hand and is using hand signals. Direct the lesson. For example, point left or right, hand up to stop, and to walk, say, 'Walk on.' If you use verbal communication, you can confuse yourself and the rider as you are facing the opposite direction from the rider.

Repeat this lesson as many times as possible. In my own lessons, I use half turns, U-turns, and zigzag to give the rider a complete experience. For example, if I want the rider to perform a U-turn, I will say, 'Keep turning, keep turning.' Remember to tell the rider to be gentle on the horse's mouth. Some riders jag at the horse's mouth.

Also explain to them the process of a complete turn. Often riders will work well for one or two strides; then they let the reins loose, and the horse walks off in another direction. This is why I use the practice turns with the parent holding the rider's hand at a standstill. If the rider is doing well off a lead rope, stop them and give them positive feedback. Then unclip the lead rope, ensuring that they see you do it. Then say who was stopping the horse. When they reply that it was you, say no.

Make them aware that it was them stopping the horse and that you were only holding the rope. This will build their confidence, giving them the confidence to ride at a walk solo. The instructor just walks in front to the side of the horse, directing tasks for the rider to undertake, such as left turn, right turn, stop, and start. Repeat until completed at a competent level. Then as the rider progresses, move on to courses that require zigzag movements.

Note: One-hour lessons are often too much for small children as they get tired. A half-an-hour lesson is sufficient. As the child progresses, stand back further and further away. This will allow them greater room to practise. To create some further excitement, make up games for the child to perform so they do not get bored from repetitive lessons. Remember, as with anything in horse riding, it is supposed to be an enjoyable experience. Finally, enjoy your riding lesson.

This is a basic stop-turn-go practice lesson. Repeat as many times as needed, ensuring that the lessons are safe. Remember, never put a beginner rider on just any horse. They are not all the same. As the rider learns, you can take the lead ride or lunge lead off the horse as the rider progresses. I usually walk in front of the beginner for the first few lessons until they learn the basic stop-go-turn. On the first part of the lesson, I keep the lead rope on the horse and walk backwards whilst giving instructions to the rider.

Note: Some people learn at different speeds and times than others. Younger children often take longer.

CLOSING REMARKS

I STARTED WRITING this book many years ago, and it has just been gathering dust, as I did not know the process involved in getting a book published. However, I went on a holiday to Malaysia, and I was telling a lady friend I had just met that I had enough information about horses to write three books. The first one is for beginners. Without my knowledge, she contacted a book publisher and started the ball rolling.

For myself, learning about horses was all hands-on working and learning over many years. However, these days, new riders are learning from TAFE courses, riding schools, pony clubs, books, and the Internet. In my day, this was not the case. I left home at the age of fourteen to start learning about horses, as from a very early age, I knew I wanted to be a jockey. My love for horses has never faded.

Even apprentice jockeys learn quicker because of modern-day courses. Trained horse people like myself have made this possible. Things have changed so much; most of my bosses could not ride a horse, so obviously they could not teach the staff. In my day, as a young jockey, you were never taught about sectionals times in horse racing. In track work, if your boss had a horse that bucked or any other bad habits, you had to ride them as you had no backup rider. As a result, I had many falls. These days, you have riders at the bigger training centres that specialise in their horses and get paid for retraining them.

This book will teach people quicker than the way I learnt. All the knowledge is here—the skills I have picked up over the years in many different countries as a rider and a trainer. Furthermore, the second and third book will have chapters involving trail riding, horse racing, teaching lessons, riding hints, basic jumping, bad horse behaviour, and correcting the problems. The follow-up books will be for more experienced horse people.

Enjoy your lesson!
Russell S. Stokes

Russell Stokes riding Karlooah after winning at Armidale.

THE END

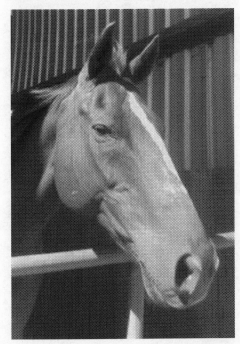

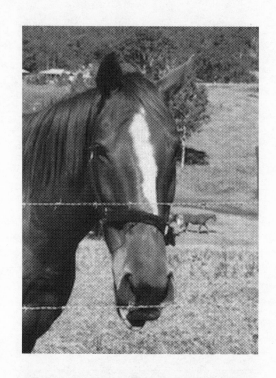

Printed in the United States
By Bookmasters